The 30-Day Writing Challenge

Begin or Enhance Your Daily Writing Habit

Sara E. Crawford

Second edition Introduction

I originally wrote The 30-Day Writing Challenge in 2014. Since that time, I have become an adjunct professor for the online creative writing graduate program at Southern New Hampshire University, I have published two novels, and I have continued four years of full-time work as a freelance writer.

I've also been through a lot of ups and down with my own publishing journey. I have been discouraged and broken down at many points. Whether you're a traditionally published author or an indie author, publishing is hard. And there's a lot of disappointment.

So much is out of your control: what the literary agents think about your writing, what the publishers think, your sales ranking on Amazon, how many reviews you have, etc. And sure, there are a ton of things you can do to increase your chances of having the agents read your manuscript or increasing your e-book sales. But as writers, the most important thing—the thing we always have control over no matter what—is the actual writing. The act of creation.

Writing is a practice and a discipline. The purpose of this book is to help you to begin a daily writing habit or enhance the daily writing habit you already have.

Whether you want to write the great American novel or write business e-books, if you are serious about being a writer, you need to practice writing every day. It's just like being in good physical shape. You have to exercise your muscles a little bit every day to build strength.

It's important to note that for some people, literally writing every day is not going to be possible. Many people have health issues that will prevent them from being able to write every day. I, myself, suffer from anxiety and depression, and there are definitely times when I'm not able to write creatively every day. (I don't think a single day has gone by in the past 15 years when I haven't written *something*, though—a journal entry, an e-mail, a blog post, web content, etc. I bring that up because if you do have mental health issues, keeping a journal is often a great way to get in some form of writing every day.)

There will also be times when life gets in the way, and writing every day isn't possible. Don't beat yourself up in these moments. The important thing is that writing becomes a regular and consistent part of your life if you want to be a writer.

Who Will Benefit From This Challenge?

This challenge will be helpful for the beginning writer as well as the writer who has worked on their craft for years. This challenge will be helpful for all types of writers: poets, writers of fiction, playwrights, screenwriters, bloggers, creative non-fiction writers, etc.

While many of these exercises can be done in multiple forms (fiction, non-fiction, poetry, script, etc.), some of the exercises ask you to use a specific form. Even if you consider yourself a fiction writer, for example, do not shy away from the poetry exercises. The purpose of this challenge is for you to step outside of your comfort zone.

For the writer who is just beginning, this challenge will help you to create a daily writing habit. Each exercise is designed to help you focus on one aspect of writing to help you perfect your craft. There are elements of every form that will help you as a writer overall—no matter what form you usually choose.

For the experienced writer, this book may be a way to stretch creatively or simply to challenge yourself. I have been writing for years, and I continue to participate in challenges like these so that I may continue to grow and develop as a writer.

If you are an experienced writer, you understand the publishing process—whether you're traditionally published or independently published—consists of a lot of waiting. You will wait for literary agents to get back to you or read your manuscript. You will wait for editors to provide you with feedback. You will wait for beta readers to finish your book and tell you their thoughts. All of this waiting around can be frustrating.

Participating in this challenge will give you an achievable goal. Work on these exercises while you are waiting for feedback, when you have writer's block, in your spare time, or when you just want to stretch your creative muscles.

Note from the Author

I would like to acknowledge that in my own writing, I constantly do the things that I say you shouldn't do. I am *far* from perfect. Every writer has room to grow and improve, and I include myself in that. However, I strive to be a better writer each and every day, and I live by these rules, principles, and ideas in my own creative life.

You should also note that while many of these ideas and exercises work wonders for me and others, every writer is different. You may find that you disagree with the way I have phrased something or a particular aspect of an exercise. You may find that the things that I describe as working for me do not work for you. And that is fine.

I am asking you to look at the big picture when you are participating in this challenge and to find the exercises and ideas that work for you. If you have to modify certain exercises to fit your style of writing, I encourage you to do so. My main goal in writing this challenge is to help writers to write more often, to write better, to write works that excite them, and to write the things that they are passionate about.

Using This Book

The best way to use this book is to schedule at least 30 minutes every day to work on the exercises. It's alright if you have to miss a day. Don't beat yourself up. Simply pick up where you left off the next day.

The first few exercises are short, and they get progressively longer as you continue. This is designed so that you can ease into your daily writing habit. However, do not feel that you have to do them in order. If you aren't feeling a particular exercise, skip it and come back to it later. Try to complete all of section one first, though, and then sections two and three, even if you have to skip around with the exercises. You may find an exercise takes you longer than one day to complete, particularly as you get to sections two and three. This is okay. The main goal of this challenge is to create a regular writing habit or to enhance the one you already have. It's not really important if it takes you 30 days or 45 days or even six months to complete this challenge as long as you work on your writing a little bit every day (or as often as you can).

This book is broken up into three sections. The first focuses on creativity and inspiration, the second focuses on writing technique, and the third encourages you to stretch your writing muscles by working with different forms and genres.

Find the system that works for you. Some people still like to use handwritten journals and notebooks whereas some people find it a lot easier to type and do their work on the computer. If you buy yourself a journal that you really love, you may be more excited about writing every day.

A lot of writers I know find they are the most productive when they get up and write first thing in the morning. Others find they are most productive in the evenings or even late at night. Find the time that works for you. Pick the same time every day and be consistent with it if you can.

Feel free to send me exercises you have been working on at sara@saracrawford.net. I would love to hear about your journey with this challenge and how it helped your writing habit.

Now that you understand a little more about this challenge and how to use it, you have all of the information you need to get going. Are you ready to go? Are you excited? Let's do it! Ready, set, write!

Section One

Creativity and Inspiration

The purpose of these exercises is simply to get you writing and flex your creativity muscles. So much of writing is giving yourself the freedom to try different things, think outside the box, and find your inspiration. Muses are everywhere. You may be inspired by an artifact you come across in a museum, a conversation you overhear at the coffee shop, or a stranger you meet while traveling abroad.

The important thing to do is to remain open to the possibilities. You may have ten ideas or even 50 before you find the one that "clicks." You will make more progress if you jot down all of your ideas and give them a chance to whirl around in your brain. It may be helpful to keep an "idea" journal or notepad with you at all times.

This section will be a great way to ease beginner writers into the writing process. For experienced writers, these exercises may help you come up with new ideas or think outside of your normal process.

Day One

Stream of Consciousness

"The scariest moment is always just before you start."
— *Stephen King*

The most important part of being a writer is actually writing. This may seem self-explanatory, but you would be surprised how many people call themselves writers without doing much writing.

In order to write anything good, you *have* to be willing to write down everything. Write down your thoughts, your feelings, your observations, your dreams, your fears, your beliefs. Any of these things may lead you to that epiphany that will lead you to that next novel, play, screenplay, or collection of poems.

I know a number of people who love books and literature but are essentially too self-conscious to write.

They are worried that whatever they write isn't going to be good. Well, this exercise is about doing the opposite. This exercise is about simply *writing*. Writing in stream of consciousness is to write down the inner monologue. Literally sit down and write everything you are thinking.

This may look something like this:

I hope that it doesn't snow. It's supposed to get to 15 degrees tonight. What is that about? This is supposed to be Georgia. I wonder what I am going to eat tonight. I will have to text Julie and see how she's doing. Why is the dog barking at no one?

Do you see how I wrote down my thoughts even though they weren't necessarily connected? It's not terribly exciting to read, but the point is just to write down your thoughts and don't censor yourself. Just keep writing no matter what. You may think this exercise is silly if you haven't done it before. You may not see the purpose. So just write about how you think it's stupid until you think of something else to write.

Stream of consciousness writing always helps me when I feel blocked. It can be a great exercise to do whether you are just starting your writing routine for the day or you are in the middle of a novel and feel stuck.

Exercise

Write in stream of consciousness for ten minutes without stopping.

Day Two

Break the Rules

"The first draft of anything is shit."— *Ernest Hemingway*

At a young playwright's festival once, one of the mentors gave us an assignment to write the absolute worst five-minute play we could. We all came up with five pages of completely melodramatic crap. We broke all of the rules of playwriting we had been taught. Not only were these plays hilarious, but they definitely helped take the pressure off and ease the tension.

This is a great exercise because as writers, we sometimes take ourselves a little too seriously (particularly in academic circles). We can be so focused on appearing to be "great writers" that we get so uptight and end up stifling the uniqueness of our own voices, our own styles.

Another problem I see for beginning writers is that they worry so much about being bad that they are afraid to write at all. If you can relate to this, you need to break out of this way of thinking as soon as possible. What better way to conquer your fear of writing something bad than to write the worst thing you can?

This exercise is a lot of fun, and I guarantee you will make yourself laugh. It takes away all of the pressure because it's *supposed* to be bad. But when you finish, you'll find that it may have just helped you have a better understanding of the "rules" you are breaking. Maybe you'll have a better understanding of how to craft exposition if you write a scene with horribly unnatural exposition. Maybe you will have a better understanding of the importance of specific imagery if you write a clichéd, sentimental poem with no imagery about how sad you are.

Exercise

Write the worst thing you can think of. Write a terrible short story, poem, or short play or screenplay around two to four pages.

When you are finished, examine your piece and ask yourself the following questions:

- What "rules" did you break to make this so bad?

- How would you do the opposite of what you did here to craft a well-written piece?

Day Three

What Do You Want To Write?

"A bird doesn't sing because it has an answer, it sings because it has a song." — *Maya Angelou*

Sometimes when I am stuck (particularly with a poem), I will take a break and write about what kind of poem I *want* to write. This often leads me to better lines than I would have gotten just by working on the poem itself. Sometimes you get so stuck in your idea of what the piece should be that you lose that spark of inspiration that made you want to write the piece in the first place.

This is also a good exercise when you are looking for ideas to begin a new novel, story, poem, play, etc. Sometimes it is good to take an inventory of the things that we believe in and value. Why do you want to be a writer? Do you want to write something that will make people laugh? Do you want to write about the human condition? Is there a political issue or cause that you believe in strongly? Thinking about these things will help you to create a credo of things that you believe in, and this will help you to come up with ideas for future projects.

Exercise

Write a 1 – 2 page list of things you believe in and things about which you would love to write. Include what kind of messages (if any) you want to convey in your writing, what the purpose of your writing is, what you hope to accomplish with your work. You may want to include a list of influences or other writers you aspire to write like.

Day Four

Leave It to Chance

"Ideas are like rabbits. You get a couple and learn how to handle them, and pretty soon you have a dozen."
— *John Steinbeck*

There is a song I wrote on my solo/acoustic album, *Unsent Letters*, called "Leave it to Chance." When I was writing this song, I knew exactly what I wanted it to be about, and I had ideas for lyrics. I didn't know what chord progression I wanted to use though. I didn't have a melody either. So I wrote down a bunch of major and minor chords and threw them in a hat. I pulled out three pieces of paper, and that became my chord progression, which helped me find a melody.

Sometimes you get a little stuck, and you need something to help you get started. This writing exercise is basically about pulling writing prompts out of a hat. This forces you to write in a way you wouldn't normally.

Exercise

1. Take three hats, bowls, or containers. One of them will be for characters, one of them will be for locations, and one of them will be for possible conflicts.

2. Write down the following list of characters on small pieces of paper:

- a homeless heroin addict

- a young inventor

- an introverted actor

- a political activist

- a depressed meteorologist

- a personal injury attorney

- an anthropology professor

- a lonely grandparent

- an astrology-obsessed psychic

- a vegetarian farmer

3. Write down the following locations on small pieces of paper:

- an island

- the streets

- the middle of nowhere in Kansas

- a large European city

- a small apartment

- a mansion

- a kitchen

- the North Pole

- Disney World

- a Broadway theatre

4. Write down the following potential conflicts on small pieces of paper:

- a hurricane is coming

- two people fight over the last piece of pizza

- an attempted theft that doesn't go as planned

- two people are stuck together

- a ghost wants to prevent someone from moving in

- someone saves their enemy's life

- someone is being chased by a bear

- technology is being hostile

- two people who hate each other have to cook a meal

5. Place all of your pieces of paper in the respective hats or bowls. Draw one character, one

location, and one potential conflict. Write a three to four page piece that somehow incorporates all three.

This forces you to be creative. For example, if you get "a depressed meteorologist," "Disney World," and "an attempted theft that doesn't go as planned," that could go so many different ways! (Someone please write that story. I want to read it!)

Day Five

Photographs

"Don't tell me the moon is shining; show me the glint of light on broken glass." — *Anton Chekhov*

Sometimes a simple image says so much, whether it's a photograph, a painting, or even an event taking place before your eyes. Have you ever seen two people embracing at the airport? Have you ever seen a bored couple sitting at a table at a restaurant, hardly speaking to each other? Have you ever watched a little kid staring at the world around him in complete awe? Did you make up stories about these people in your head when you saw them?

This is an example of using your imagination to create a story based on an image, which is exactly what I'm asking you to do here.

Exercise

Visit http://writingexercises.co.uk/random-image-generator.php and generate a random image. Look at it for at least five minutes without writing anything. What does the image make you think of? What does the image make you feel? What is the story behind the image? What's going on behind the camera or behind the scenes? What can you not see?

After you reflect, write a three to five page piece based on your reflections.

Day Six

The Found Poem

"Good writers borrow, great writers steal." --T.S. Eliot

Found poetry is like making a collage with words. When text from one source is broken up, cut out, and rearranged, a found poem is created. Found poems are a lot of fun, and they bring a new perspective to a text. They will also help you to pay attention to the words and phrases you use and how you arrange them.

I did this exercise once and ended up writing a found poem comprised of text I found on the raunchiest Craigslist personal ads. The text I started with was often poorly written, overly sexual, and even surreal at times. When I composed a poem from these ads, though, it became this sad and lonely call for something greater.

I encourage you to look through text you wouldn't ordinarily read. Find an interesting webpage or pick up a random book at the library. Fashion magazines, recipe books, and e-mails all work extremely well.

Don't worry so much about the art of poetry right now. Just focus on taking words and phrases out of context and arranging them into something new. Pay attention to the way you arrange the words and phrases to compose your new poem and the new perspective you gain.

Exercise

Write a found poem no more than one page in length using text from another source such as a magazine article, a book, a webpage, a blog post, etc.

Day Seven

Let the Music Move You

"Don't forget the songs that made you cry

And the songs that saved your life." -- *Morrissey*

Music shapes the way I see the world. I am always making mixes (I call them "mixies") depending on what season it is (the "Scent of Autumn" mixy) or how I feel or what I'm doing (the "Driving Downtown to the Show By Myself" mixy). When I am working on a novel or a play, I usually make playlists for particular characters, scenes, overall themes, etc. Music can be a real inspiration for writers.

Music can touch you, move you in a way that no other art can. Music transports you back in time, making you remember things vividly. Music inspires new ideas and feelings and stories and characters. Music can be incredibly powerful if you let it.

When I was writing my novel, *We Own the Sky,* I had trouble connecting with a particular character, and all of his scenes felt a little flat. I also felt I wasn't developing him in the way that I wanted to. I made a list of all of the bands I thought he would like (many of which I hadn't spent a lot of time listening to in the past), and I listened to one particular album over and over. It brought me a new understanding of this character, and I found that I not only felt connected to this character, but I *wanted* to write more about him, which allowed me to be able to develop him in a more efficient way.

What I'm asking you to do in this exercise is allow a piece of music to move you and inspire you.

Exercise

Put your music collection on shuffle or open up an internet radio station on Spotify or Pandora. *Listen* to the next song that plays without writing anything. Notice whatever feelings the song brings up in you. Notice any thoughts that pass through your mind.

When the song is over, grab your journal and do some free writing. Answer the following questions:

- How did the song make you feel? Melancholy, excited, irritated, angry?

- Did the song remind you of anyone or anything? Who? What?

- What do you think the song is about? What do you think the song means?

When you have answered those questions, see if your free writing could lead you to a story. Write down any characters, situations, or images that come to mind. (Variation: Do this exercise with three different songs.)

Day Eight

See Some ART!

"For it would seem - her case proved it - that we write, not with the fingers, but with the whole person. The nerve which controls the pen winds itself about every fibre of our being, threads the heart, pierces the liver."
— *Virginia Woolf*

All artists need to experience other forms of art. Whether it's a play, a film, a painting, a sculpture, a poem, a novel, or a song, art inspires us to become better artists ourselves. For example, when I go see a complex or provocative play, I may get home and want to immediately write a song. When I see a captivating band performing in a local dive bar, it may make me think of a really great character I want to explore in a novel.

Art has the capacity to inspire us, to move us. Even if you go to a performance that is absolutely awful or boring, you may want to go home and write about why it was so boring. All art can teach us something.

I think it's incredibly important for artists to support other local and independent artists. When you attend these events, you are saying to these artists, "I believe in what you are doing. You have a voice, and I want to hear what you have to say." It could be that particular artist is having one of those "Why am I doing this and why don't I just go work at McDonald's? I hate my life" days that we *all* have as artists and your comments will give her a reason to want to do what she does for another day.

For the purposes of this exercise, I'm going to talk about visual art, but I think it's equally important to support local music, theatre, literary events, films, etc.

when you can. Typically, these events are cheap or even free. (And there are always ways to attend for free. For example, if you volunteer to usher at a performance, you will get to see it for free.) See what events you can attend and what local artists you can support.

Exercise

Go see some visual art. Find a local art gallery that has an exhibit, go to your local college or community center and see if they have anything on display, and/or Google art events in your area. If the event is happening later, write it down on your calendar and complete this exercise by observing a random piece of art on a website like deviantART or flickr.

Look at the piece of visual art and study it for a moment. What does this piece make you feel? What does it remind you of? In your opinion, what did the artist intend to express?

Free write in your journal for at least 1-2 pages about the piece of art. Jot down any characters or storylines it inspires you to imagine.

Day Nine

Connect with the Outside World

"We write to taste life twice, in the moment and in retrospect." — *Anaïs Nin*

When I am stuck as a writer, going for a walk almost *always* helps me. There is something about being outside and feeling connected to the trees, the wind, the scurrying squirrels, and even the crawling insects that clears my head and allows me to get *ideas*. When I was writing *We Own the Sky*, I would go for 45 minute to one hour walks in the park listening to my favorite Muse songs and when I would return to my desk, I would be full of new ideas. Sometimes I would have to even jot some down in the car on the way home from the park.

Connecting with nature gives me perspective and makes me feel both small and a part of something greater at the same time. I highly recommend this not just for times when you are stuck as a writer but for times when you are stuck *as a person.* If things feel overwhelming or you are incredibly stressed out, just go for a walk. Even if it's a short walk, it will make you feel better.

If you live in an urban area, you may not be able to connect with nature by walking outside, but you can connect with the busy sidewalks, the buzzing streets, the concrete buildings, and the busy people passing by. There are so many things that can potentially be your next Muse. All you have to do is be willing to see them.

Going outside is a natural way of nourishing the creative mind. If you typically get a lot of ideas, you may see any number of interesting things by taking a quick walk. Even if you live in a rural area and there are no people around, you may see a particular tree that makes you feel a certain way or gives you an idea. Inspiration is everywhere.

Exercise

Go for a walk for ten minutes. If you cannot do this, find a window and look outside for ten minutes. Do not write anything down. Just look, observe, and see what comes up in you.

After the ten minutes have passed, pull out your journal and free write for ten to 20 minutes about the experience. What did you see? Describe your surroundings in detail. Describe everything that happened. Did you get any ideas? What is your relationship to this place? How does this place make

you feel?

Day Ten

Write in an Unusual Place

"Writer's block is a fancy term made up by whiners so they can have an excuse to drink alcohol." — Steve Martin

How many of us have routines, going to the same places and seeing the same people every day? Some of us like stability and having a normal routine. This is productive for many people, even creative types. However, it can sometimes be stifling. Sometimes it makes us feel stuck.

Have you ever taken a completely different route on your way home from work just because you wanted to see something different? Have you ever tried a new restaurant or gone to see a movie you knew nothing about?

Trying new things is an important thing to do for anyone. For the writer, it is essential. You should always challenge yourself to have new experiences, see new things, and try different things. That is what this exercise is about. You see things differently when you write in an unusual place.

Exercise

Go to a new place that is not somewhere you usually go to write. If you are able to go to another physical place—like a coffee shop or café you have never been—go there. You could also try writing in Laundromats, libraries, public parks, museums, the lobby of a movie theatre, the post office, a church, the bar, or the mall. Get creative. I'm sure there are tons of places where you have never written.

If you cannot go to another location, try writing in a different room or part of living space. Do you ever write in the bath tub? Do you ever write in the kitchen? Do you ever write on your front porch or in the fitness center of your apartment building? Go to some place that is an "unusual" writing place.

Write a short story, poem, short play, or short screenplay that begins with the line, "She said you would be here." There is no suggested length for this exercise.

Section Two: Technique

Now that you have been working on inspiration, developing ideas, and creating a daily writing habit (or enhancing the one you already have), it's time to focus on technique. In this section, we will explore ten tools that great writers often use. It should be said that creative writers often break the rules in order to tell the story they need to tell. However, breaking the rules is much more effective if you understand them.

For the next ten exercises, work on the assigned topic regardless of how often you plan to use that specific tool. You never know when you will subconsciously use something you learned about the "rules of creative writing."

Some of these things will be useful and some may be less useful, but the act of doing the exercises will make you a stronger writer because you are working on your craft and your technique. If this were a physical workout, section one was all about stretching your muscles and being flexible to encourage creativity. Section two is the muscle strength training section. So get ready to do some writer push-ups and squats!

Day Eleven

Plot Structure and Outlining

"There is no rule on how to write. Sometimes it comes easily and perfectly; sometimes it's like drilling rock and then blasting it out with charges." — *Ernest Hemingway*

Some writers like to make meticulous outlines and lists before they even start. Some writers like to just start and see what happens. There is no "right" way to do things. However, getting familiar with the outline and the way many stories are structured is beneficial. Sometimes when I am stuck, I might try outlining in different ways. For example, once I took a bunch of colored index cards and wrote down everything I thought should happen in my novel. Then, I spread them out over the coffee table. Simply looking at everything that way helped me to decide the order of events and it helped me to see a couple of new events that were missing.

Outlining is a good way to see the overall structure of your work. Let's look two common structures we may see in literature:

Dramatic Structure

The dramatic structure is typically used in plays and films, but it can also apply to novels. It originated in Aristotle's *Poetics* and it consists of:

- Exposition – The main characters are introduced and the central conflict is presented.

- Complicating or Rising Action – The conflict increases, which propels the plot forward, and the characters are developed further.

- <u>Climax</u> – This is the turning point. There is no turning back after this event as it changes the fate of the protagonist or the story overall.

- <u>Falling Action</u> – The conflict unravels and the story begins to conclude.

- <u>Dénouement</u> – This is the resolution of the story. Conflicts are resolved. By the end, the protagonist is changed in some way. Usually, in comedies, he or she is better off than at the beginning of the story, and in tragedies, he or she is worse off than at the beginning.

The Hero's Journey

Joseph Campbell argues that all myths and many other types of stories have the same general structure, which he calls the Hero's Journey:

- <u>Ordinary World</u> – This is the "regular" life of the protagonist before the story begins.

- <u>Call to Adventure</u> – Something makes the protagonist begin his or her adventure. The protagonist may be presented with a challenge or a problem he/she has to solve.

- <u>Refusal of the Call</u> – The protagonist tries to refuse the call to adventure.

- <u>Meeting with the Mentor</u> – The protagonist connects with a wiser person who can give advice and wisdom for the adventure.

- <u>Crossing the First Threshold</u> – The protagonist leaves his or her regular life behind and encounters the first threshold of the adventure.

- <u>Tests, Allies, Enemies</u> – The hero meets allies and friends as well as enemies. He or she is tested as he or she becomes familiar with the new world.

- <u>Approach</u> - There may be obstacles or setbacks that cause the hero to use a different approach to the situation.

- <u>Ordeal</u> – A major crisis occurs. This may include the death of someone close to the protagonist.

- <u>Reward</u> – The protagonist survives and overcomes all obstacles, achieving his or her goal.

- <u>The Road Back</u> – The protagonist starts to journey back to the ordinary world.

- <u>Resurrection Hero</u> – A final test is given to the protagonist, forcing him/her to use the knowledge he/she has gained.

- <u>Return with Elixir</u> – The hero returns to the ordinary world, but he/she is now a changed and better person because of what he/she has learned.

Exercise

Take one of the plot structures we discussed and create an outline for a story based on that structure. You may use this in the future, and you may not. The point in this exercise is to focus on structuring a story and creating an outline that sticks to one of these plot structures.

Day Twelve

Word Choice

"Writers fish for the right words like fishermen fish for, um, whatever those aquatic creatures with fins and gills are called." — *Jarod Kintz*

While it is nice to know a lot of fancy words, being a good writer does not necessarily mean having an expansive vocabulary. A good writer knows how to choose the *right* words.

I have a decent vocabulary, but I didn't do very well on the **GRE** vocabulary section. Sure, it's fun to get a word of the day in your e-mail inbox and learn new words daily. I think that the challenge for most writers, though, is often using the same words to describe things. (If you've ever written a novel or a longer work and then performed a search to discover you used the word "ridiculous" 25 times, you'll know what I mean.)

Expanding your vocabulary is a helpful thing to do, but I think it's more beneficial to practice using words you don't normally use. This will help you to find the right word. You may get to a line in your poem when a girl has a melancholy look on her face. And you may discover that "melancholy" isn't *quite* the word you were looking for. Does she have desolate look on her face? Is it a downcast look? Gloomy? Sorrowful? Morose? Is there a better word you can use to describe the look on her face?

Exercise

Write a piece of no more than 4 pages. Use all of the following words:

- animosity

- empowered

- aquamarine

- quotable

- drifter

- bewitching

- willow

- passion

- serene

- rejuvenated

Variation: Use a random word generator like the one at Text Finder - http://www.textfixer.com/tools/random-words.php to complete the exercise.

Day Thirteen – Character

"Which of us has not felt that the character we are reading in the printed page is more real than the person standing beside us?" — *Cornelia Funke*

Characters are what make the story. It's lovely to have unusual plots and concepts, but even the most successful science fiction, for example, is successful because there are well-defined and well-developed characters. These characters are three-dimensional, they have flaws and passions, and they seem like living, breathing people.

Writing a three-dimensional character is often challenging. When I am figuring out who my characters are, I think back to the times when I have done theatre. I always wrote a lot about the characters I was playing–their back stories, what kind of music they liked, their hopes and aspirations, their flaws, their pet peeves, the details that made them who they were. These visceral details really helped me to get to know who they were, which (hopefully) helped me in my portrayal of them.

I think it's even more important to get to know your characters intimately when you create them from scratch. Find out what he likes, what he doesn't like, who he voted for in the last election. Find out where he comes from. Find out who his friends are, who his family is, whether he has any friends at all. And sure, you don't have to use all of the information that you come up with in the story. Maybe the fact that your character's favorite ice cream flavor is strawberry is not important in a story about how she is trying to kill aliens. However, it may be important for you as the writer to know that her favorite ice cream flavor is strawberry. Maybe that tiny detail will affect a decision she makes. Or maybe it won't. But it's another aspect of her personality that you know.

Exercise

Think of a character. Answer all of the following questions about this character:

- Where did they grow up?

- What was their childhood like? What is their family like?

- What are their ambitions, dreams, and goals?

- What are their political and religious beliefs?

- What kind of person are they attracted or drawn to?

- What is their favorite book? Movie? Band or music? TV show?

- What kind of clothes do they wear?

- What is their favorite food?

- What do they look like?

- What are they the most passionate about?

- What are their strengths and weaknesses?

- What makes them feel annoyed or irritated?

- What makes them feel happy? Sad? Angry?

- What do they love to do on the weekends?

Day Fourteen

Varied Sentence Structure

"I write to find out what I'm talking about." — *Edward Albee*

Having a varied sentence structure is an important aspect of writing. It sounds repetitive if you use a lot of simple, short sentences. *He grabbed the keys. He drove the car. He went home.* It also becomes repetitive if you overuse long, complex sentences. *He picked up the keys, and gripped them tightly in his hand before opening the car door and slumping down in the driver seat. He turned the key in the ignition and checked the rearview mirror carefully before he accelerated onto the street to meet the day.* You want to make sure you are varying your sentence structure so that you have a balance of simple and complex sentences.

Another mistake many writers make is starting every sentence the same way. *He grabbed the keys and got in the car. He kept his eyes on the road and turned up the radio. He started singing along to his favorite song.* A better way to write this would be something like: *He grabbed the keys and got into his car. Turning up the radio, he kept his eyes on the road ahead. When "1979" by the Smashing Pumpkins came on, he couldn't help but sing along.* In this example, the sentences are more varied, and each sentence begins a different way.

Different sentences may be better for different purposes. For example, if you are writing from the point of view of a character that is having a very manic, scatter-brained moment, you may want to have choppier, shorter sentences.

Overall, though, it's important to be aware of sentence variation and to make sure that you are not repetitive.

Exercise

Write a fictional paragraph. It can be about anything.

Take that same paragraph and re-write it. Use different types of sentences, and pay attention to the sentences you are using. How does the second version differ from the original? Is it more effective?

Re-write the paragraph a second time. Use a different combination of sentence types and make sure the beginnings of your sentences are varied. How does this version differ? Is it more or less effective?

Which version of the paragraph accomplishes your purpose the most?

Day Fifteen

Dialogue

"Write what disturbs you, what you fear, what you have not been willing to speak about. Be willing to be split open." — *Natalie Goldberg*

The way a person speaks is as unique as his or her fingerprints. If you go to a coffee shop and listen to people talking, you will quickly realize that everyone has a different tone and a different way of speaking. Everyone has their own way of phrasing things. The way a character speaks can reveal her cultural background, where she is from, how much education she has had, and many more aspects of who she is as a person.

One thing I like to do when I'm revising is make sure that each character has a unique sound. In playwriting workshops, my professors always told me that you should be able to look at a line of dialogue and know who is speaking just by reading the line and not looking at the character's name. This helps to make your characters sound distinctive.

This is also a good exercise for fiction. If you are writing in first person, does your narrator speak the way he thinks? Perhaps he uses a lot of explicit words in his inner dialogue but tries to present himself as being proper when he speaks. Already, you have told us a ton about who this guy is just by the tone of his dialogue versus the tone of his inner dialogue. Pay attention to the way your characters speak and how they say what they say.

Exercise

Go to a public place like a coffee shop. The airport is great for this exercise. Bring your journal with you. Sit in one place and *listen* to the way people speak as opposed to what they say. Pay attention to dialect. Do they pronounce certain words differently? What can you infer about them just by listening to the way they speak?

Jot down different phrases and word that you find interesting. Why do you find these phrases interesting? What can you infer about the characters by looking at these phrases?

Day Sixteen

Revision

"Write with the door closed, rewrite with the door open."— *Stephen King, On Writing*

Writing the first draft of any story is a fun and creative process. Most of the magic happens, though, when you revise. I think of a first draft as a slab of marble. There is much work to be done before it becomes a sculpture. I know many writers who are always striving to write that perfect first draft so they won't have to do any revisions.

Revisions have gotten a bad rap. Many of my writer friends have told me that revising is their least favorite part of the process. I *love* revisions, though. If you're doing it right, revisions can be the most creative part.

When you have a first draft, you have the meat of the story you are trying to tell. When you look back and start revising, it's like putting together a puzzle. You have to figure out how all of the pieces can come together to get the story you have in your head onto the page in the best way possible.

Feedback is crucial for the writing process. It's important to have objective opinions about what works and what doesn't work so that you can fix the things that don't work and expand upon the things that do.

What kind of feedback should you get? It really depends on the purpose of your writing. If you have a short story, and you simply want to improve it, send it to some honest friends or family members who are avid readers. If you have written a novel, and you want to get a literary agent or get published, it would be worth it to pay a professional editor to give you constructive criticism and feedback. There are also many resources online where you can get feedback from other writers.

Whether you get feedback from friends, family, teachers, professional editors, or fellow writers, the best thing to do is to read or hear the feedback without emotional reactions. Do not argue with the notes or criticism. Do not even say anything. Just listen to or read the notes and process them.

Once you have gotten feedback, you usually want to give it some time to sink in. You may want to wait a day or two. You may want to wait a few weeks. It just depends. But think about the notes and give the piece some space.

Come back to your piece with a fresh set of eyes. The great thing about being the writer is that you don't have to use every piece of criticism you receive. When you hear or read the criticism, you will know which notes are helpful and which notes to ignore. The notes that inspire you to think of new possibilities and ideas are the ones to keep.

The most important thing to keep in mind is not to take it personally. Every first draft needs to be improved and revised quite a bit. No one is saying you are unintelligent or a bad writer. Try to disassociate yourself from the work. This is harder said than done, I know. Fortunately, I have *a lot* of experience with criticism so I have gotten reasonably good at receiving it. But it's essential to make sure that you don't let the fear of criticism stop you from writing. And at the end of the day, you need to remember that another person's opinion is just that: another person's opinion.

Revision is all about re-imaging your piece and trying new things. Is there a new way you can say what you're trying to say? Are there new situations your characters need to get themselves into? Is there a new way to get from one important plot point to another?

Is there an additional scene you need to add? Do you need to cut down nonessential information to make it flow better? These are all important questions to answer when you are revising.

Exercise

For the sake of keeping this a "one day" exercise, there probably won't be time to seek external feedback. For this exercise, you will have to give yourself some feedback.

Take a look at one of the exercises you have already completed in this challenge. Read it with objective eyes, as if someone else wrote it. What really works about this piece? What doesn't work about this piece? What are the strengths of the work? How might it be improved? Does anything need to be added? Is everything that is there essential to the story, poem, play, etc.?

With those questions in mind, revise or re-write your piece.

Day Seventeen

Point of View

"Writing is a socially acceptable form of schizophrenia."

— *E.L. Doctorow*

There are many different ways to tell a story. You can tell a story from first person point of view in past tense (i.e. "I woke up and went to the store."), third person point of view – limited (i.e. "She woke up and went to the store."), third person omniscient (i.e. "She woke up and went to the store, and she wasn't very happy about it."), second person (i.e. "You woke up and went to the store.") and a whole other variety of options.

How you choose to tell a story is just as important as what actually happens in a story. You can have a complex and provocative plot, but if you don't use the best point of view, it may not come across. Here are a few questions you may want to ask yourself before deciding on a point of view.

Past or Present – How do you want the story to be revealed? Do you want to use past tense or present tense? Past tense implies that some time has gone by and the narrator is reflecting back to tell the story. This may change the way the story is told. For example, it's unlikely that the main character dies if the story is being told in first person, past tense. (Not impossible, but unlikely.) If a story is in present tense, that makes the reader feel like she is in the middle of the action. I thought *The Hunger Games* by Suzanne Collins was a great use of present tense, for example, because the reader was right there with Katniss, wondering if she was going to survive.

Omniscient or Limited – Who's side are you on?
Do you want your readers to know the thoughts and
emotions of one character, all characters, or no
characters? Is the narrator an objective party that has
his own thoughts and beliefs? I thought *The Book
Thief* by Markus Zusak had a very creative use of
point of view. Telling a World War II/Holocaust story
from the perspective of Death was a brilliant decision.
One thing to remember is that the reader may have
more sympathy for a character whose thoughts and
emotions are known. This is not always true, of
course, but aren't you more likely to sympathize with
someone when you understand why they are behaving
the way that they are?

Reliable or Unreliable – Is your character telling
the truth? Sometimes it can be really entertaining and
rewarding to read a story from the point of view of an
unreliable narrator. One of the most famous

unreliable narrators in the coming of age genre would certainly be Holden Caulfield in J.D. Salinger's *Catcher in the Rye*. Of course, you could argue that any first person narrator is unreliable. Everyone tells a story with his or her own perspective, and that might not exactly match up with someone else's perspective. If a car accident happens, for example, ten people can see it and tell you ten different versions of the same event. Nevertheless, it's important to think about how reliable your narrator should be.

Exercise

Write one page of fiction where two characters have a conflict about something. Write the story from one point of view. It can be in first person, third person, etc. (It doesn't matter if the conflict is resolved or if the story has a beginning, middle, and end.)

Re-write the same story from a different point of view. You can do first person and switch to the other character. You can do third person instead of first or first instead of third. Additionally, you can switch from past to present or present to past.

Look at your two versions of the same story. How did switching the point of view affect the way the story was told? What did you gain? What did you lose?

Day Eighteen

Foreshadowing

"Unintentional foreshadowing is unintentionally hilarious."— *Sarah Wendell*

Foreshadowing—a way of providing the reader with hints or clues of what's going to happen—is a great tool when used properly. Foreshadowing can add tension to your story and make it more interesting. Because it creates suspense, is especially important in mysteries and thrillers, but it is also important in other types of writing. It can be subtle like when there are dark clouds or an eerie atmosphere before a murder or it can be more direct like when Romeo and Juliet discuss how they do not want to live without each other.

You can create foreshadowing in a play, a story, a film, or even a poem in many different ways. For example, if you see a shot of someone holding a gun in a movie, there is a good chance that someone is going to get shot by the end of the movie. You can create foreshadowing by describing a change in the weather or the general mood in the atmosphere. You can give your characters dialogue that will hint at events to come. You can describe objects in a specific way that hints at upcoming events.

There are a number of ways that you can use this tool. One way to think about foreshadowing is to go back to the last book that you loved. Think about the climax or the big "event" in the book. Were there any hints that this was going to occur? Did the characters say anything in the dialogue that may have clued in the reader? Were there shifts in mood or in the weather?

One of the most beneficial ways to learn about writing is to examine books that you love. Analyze the tools the writers have used to tell the stories, and try to emulate them to tell your stories.

Exercise

Write a one-page piece where someone is murdered by the end. Go back to the beginning and see how you can foreshadow this death at the beginning of the story. Think about the dialogue, the objects, and the weather. Think about your descriptions and your tone. How can you insert clues and hints for the reader without making it obvious?

Day Nineteen

Research

"There is creative reading as well as creative writing."
— *Ralph Waldo Emerson*

Being a good writer involves doing research. With genres like historical fiction, this is quite obvious. Even with other genres, though, you may need to do research. For example, if you have a character that loves soccer, and you aren't much of a soccer enthusiast, you need to read articles, look at websites, and watch some videos to learn the ins and outs of the sport. You will then be able to convincingly write from the point of view of a soccer fan. If you read an interesting news article that inspires you, fleshing out your idea will often require further research.

Research doesn't just mean Googling information or going to the library. Your research may require you to interview people, watch films, listen to radio programs or podcasts, or visit different locations. It depends on how involved you want to get. If you live in New Orleans and you want to write a novel that takes place in San Francisco, you may want to go to San Francisco to get a feel for the city.

But don't worry. You don't have to physically go to a location to write a story that takes place there. Stephenie Meyer had never been to Forks, Washington before she set her *Twilight* series there. Say what you will about *Twilight,* but the series had an excellent sense of place. The city of Forks became another character in the series. It's possible to do all of the research you need to do on the internet. It's important that you get involved in whatever way you can, and learn everything you can about your subject.

Exercise

Go to a news website or get a newspaper and read a news article that speaks to you. Try to pick a news article that features something with which you are unfamiliar. Maybe the news story has taken place in a location you haven't visited, maybe the article features someone in a profession you are unfamiliar with, etc. Do some research on the aspect of the news story with which you are unfamiliar. Do internet research, listen to related podcasts, go to the library and flip through relevant books. If there is anyone you can contact for more information, do so.

Write a short piece of two to four pages that includes some aspect of your research.

Day Twenty

Completion

"Sometimes writing is running downhill, your fingers jerking behind you on the keyboard the way your legs do when they can't quite keep up with gravity." —

Rainbow Rowell, Fangirl

You may have wonderful, three-dimensional characters. You may have engaging and unique dialogue. You may have fabulous foreshadowing, varied sentence structure, excellent word usage, and so on. You can have all of these things, though, and not have a complete story.

The simplest way to figure out if you have a complete story is to ask, "Does this story have a beginning, middle, and end?" This sounds simple. "Of course my story has a beginning, middle, and end!" you might say. Sometimes, though, as writers, we can get so caught up in all of the fancy things we are doing and our stories lack the necessary beginning, middle, and end. Let's examine each of these three elements:

- **Beginning** - The beginning includes an introduction of characters and an introduction of the main conflict. There should be some event that is called the inciting incident that leads to the rest of the events in the story.

- **Middle** - In the middle of the story, there are complications and the conflict increases. This is where we learn more about the characters and reach a climax.

- **End** - The story comes to a conclusion, and the main conflict is resolved.

For many writers, the end is the hardest part. In playwriting, we always talk about how Act Two is the most difficult to write. You may have a great idea for a story with intriguing characters and conflict that is full of tension, but you have no idea how it ends. Or you may know how it ends but not how to get there.

There are different ways that writers can find the conclusion of their stories. You may have to try different things before you find the method that works for you. You might try just writing until you figure out what happens. You might write out several endings until you find the right one that works for you.

Exercise

Writing the end can be difficult if you have a tendency to start projects and not complete them. In this case, we have a hard time coming up with endings because we don't have a lot of practice writing endings.

Write out three different sets of beginnings, middles, and endings for three different stories. The main purpose of this exercise is to practice coming up with the best way to resolve a story so focus on making the ending fitting to the rest of the story.

Section Three

Exploring Different Forms and Genres

Now that you have practiced different ways to come up with ideas and you have also worked on several aspects that will improve your technique, it's time to really get your hands dirty. The following exercises will ask you to stretch outside of your comfort zone as each exercise will focus on a different genre or form. I ask that you stay open minded. If you are primarily a poet, do not shy away from the screenwriting exercise. If you are primarily a writer of nonfiction, challenge yourself to complete the poetry exercise.

Each form of writing has a great deal to teach us. You may not be destined to be a professional playwright, but by practicing the art of playwriting, it may help you with your fiction. Every genre has something to teach you as well. Fantasy and sci-fi can encourage you to be more imaginative, for example. Mystery requires you to plan your entire plot beforehand. Horror or erotica may require you to push yourself beyond your comfort zone and take risks. We will not get to all of these genres of writing, but we will explore a few.

You may find that you enjoy one of these exercises so much, you want to write more in that form in the future. It may inspire you to read more in that particular genre. My hope is that these exercises will expand your horizons as a writer and help you to become a better-rounded artist.

Are you ready? It's almost the home stretch! You've gotten this far so let's finish it up!

Day Twenty-One

Honesty (Non-fiction)

"And by the way, everything in life is writable about if you have the outgoing guts to do it, and the imagination to improvise. The worst enemy to creativity is self-doubt."

— Sylvia Plath

It's important to be honest as a writer. You may think this is a contradiction. How can we be honest when we are creating a work of fiction? Isn't the act of telling a story an act of lying? Yes and no. Technically, when you write fiction, you are making stuff up. However, you can still be true to yourself, true to your characters, true to the situations, and true to the prominent themes in the works that you create, and this requires honesty. This requires being able to stand up against critics and sometimes even readers.

Why do you need to stand up to readers? Aren't you writing for the readers? Yes and no. Different writers have different opinions on this. Obviously, writers like George R.R. Martin care a lot more about being true to the story than making their readers happy. Other writers seem to be afraid to do *anything* their readers don't like. I think it's best to be somewhere in the middle. J.K. Rowling is a good example. If she would have done what made readers happy, no one would have died in the *Harry Potter* series except perhaps Voldemort, which would have been nice, but it wouldn't have accurately conveyed how high the stakes were in the world she created.

Writing non-fiction is a great way to practice being honest as writers. Some people think "creative non-fiction" is a contradiction in and of itself. How can you be creative about writing a story that comes from real life? In creative non-fiction, you are telling the truth and being creative with the words you choose, the way you frame the story, and other devices you may use. Just because you are being truthful does not mean you can't be creative in the way you craft the story as a writer.

Exercise

Write a short story from your life about a time that you took a risk. This could be when you asked your first crush to dance at the middle school dance, when you drove drunk that one night, when you gambled a lot of money, when you went on a job interview, etc. Be creative.

Day Twenty-Two

Imagery (Poetry)

"Poetry is just the evidence of life. If your life is burning well, poetry is just the ash." — *Leonard Cohen*

Good poems are full of memorable images. Instead of just saying "I feel sad" in a poem, give the reader an image that makes *them* feel sad. The most famous poem used to teach poetry students about the power of imagery is William Carlos Williams's poem "The Red Wheelbarrow":

The Red Wheelbarrow

so much depends

upon

a red wheel

barrow

glazed with rain

water

beside the white

chickens.

Here, Williams give us a very powerful image. Can't you just *see* that? The "red wheelbarrow glazed with rainwater beside the white chickens" pops out and sticks with you. William Wordsworth said that poetry is the "spontaneous overflow of emotion recollected in tranquility." It's easy for us writers to get the "spontaneous overflow of emotion" down but do we always recollect in tranquility? In the case of poetry, part of recollecting in tranquility requires the crafting of powerful images to express the spontaneous overflow of emotion you feel.

Exercise

Do some free writing about the last time you felt
an overwhelming emotion, whether it's fear, sadness,
anger, giddiness, love, loneliness, nostalgia, etc. Take a
look at that free writing and turn that emotion into a
poem with three to five memorable images that
express that emotion.

Day Twenty-Three

Subtext (Playwriting)

"I write entirely to find out what I'm thinking, what I'm looking at, what I see and what it means. What I want and what I fear." — *Joan Didion*

In real life, people don't always say what they mean. So why would your characters? One of the most significant aspects to writing a good play is writing good, sharp dialogue. Most plays—particularly in black box theatres or smaller theatres—do not depend on many scene changes, special effects, or other grandiose storytelling devices that film and television use. It's very popular in a play to have two or three characters on stage in one setting for the entire act, if not the entire play. In these cases, it's essential for playwrights to craft interesting dialogue that will keep the audience engaged.

One of the best ways to write better dialogue is to think about the subtext. Subtext is the text underneath the lines explicitly spoken by a character. To find the subtext, look at a line a character is saying and ask yourself the following questions:

- Why is the character saying this?

- What do they really mean?

- What are they trying to accomplish by saying that?

Let's take a look at a brief conversation from one of my short plays, *The Economist.*

DARCIE
Yeah. Hey, so, I talked to my sister today.

WILL
Did you?

DARCIE

She told me to tell you hey. (WILL nods.) And, you know, I'm going back to Memphis for Christmas if you... you know... want to come with me.

WILL

I don't know. I'm very busy at the office.

DARCIE

So, I guess you heard. About the wedding. (WILL doesn't say anything.) He's a nice guy. She's really happy with him. (Pause) I'm... sorry. You don't want me to, like, move out now, do you?

WILL

No, why would you think that?

DARCIE

I kind of thought the only reason you were letting me stay here is because you're still... sort of... in love with my sister.

WILL

No. That was a long time ago.

DARCIE

Right... Okay... Yeah.

Let's take a look at the same conversation, except that now I will give you the subtext of each line in bold.

DARCIE

Yeah. Hey, so, I talked to my sister today. **(This is going to be awkward.)**

WILL

Did you? **(I need to act nonchalant, like I don't care.)**

DARCIE

She told me to tell you hey. (WILL nods.) And, you know, I'm going back to Memphis for Christmas if you...you know...want to come with me. **(How much does he know? I will feel him out.)**

WILL

I don't know. I'm very busy at the office. **(I can't go home and watch the love of my life marry some other guy.)**

DARCIE

So, I guess you heard. About the wedding. (WILL doesn't say anything.) He's a nice guy. She's really happy with him. **(Ugh. I just wish he was over my sister already!)** (Pause) I'm... sorry. You don't want me to, like, move out now, do you?

WILL

No, why would you think that? **(Where is that coming from?)**

DARCIE

I kind of thought the only reason you were letting me stay here is because you're still... sort of... in love with my sister. **(It's really obvious.)**

WILL
No. That was a long time ago. (Well, I *shouldn't* still be in love with her, anyway.)

DARCIE
Right... Okay... Yeah. (Yeah. I'm totally convinced.)

See how that works? There is subtext underneath almost everything we say as people, and understanding the subtext in your characters' dialogue will help you to understand your characters in a much better way.

Exercise

Write a short play or scene of a play of four to five pages. Keep the characters at a minimum of three and make sure there is some conflict. Once you have the scene written, go back through it and write the subtext of each line as I did above. Use the proper play script formatting as shown above.

Day Twenty-Four

Narration (Fiction)

"Writing is the only thing that when I do it, I don't feel I should be doing something else." — *Gloria Steinem*

In fiction, we can get deep into a character's brain in a way that we can't in other mediums. Fiction can be the best medium for thoughtful observations and narrations. In fiction, we can go deep into a character's thoughts and feelings and get to know a character by the way he or she interacts with the world.

Fiction gives us a certain intimacy with characters that we might not get from films or plays. We get to see the complex layers that make up a person. Think about your own life and how many layers there are to your thoughts and experiences. You are the only person who fully understands all of the subtext, symbolism, and complex beauty of your own life, the events that happen to you, and the way you have grown and developed.

When we write fiction, the goal is to create characters that also have those complex layers and make them seem as real as possible so that we can tell their stories. We do this for many different reasons. Some people write fiction to entertain. Some people write fiction to explore a universal aspect of humanity. Some people write fiction to tell stories that need to be told to express a deeper truth about the human condition. Whatever the reason, writing fiction is a great way to practice constructing a complex character with many layers.

Exercise

Go back to your Character exercise from "Day Thirteen." Use the information you discovered about that character and write a short story from his or her point of view (first person or third person) and use more narration including inner thoughts and feelings than dialogue or action. It's okay if the story doesn't have a beginning, middle, and end. Focus on the complex layers that make up the character and try to give the reader a level of intimacy with that character.

Day Twenty-Five

Visualization (Screenwriting)

"The way you write a screenplay is that you close your eyes and run the movie in your head and then you write it down."— Salman Rushdie

If you have written a good screenplay, readers should be able to *see* the movie as they read. Films are a visual medium. While it's true that many films are more theatrical and have a strong focus on dialogue as in plays, the best films are those that use the medium to its full advantage. You can do so many things in a film that you can't do in a play. You can *show* the audience so many things that you can't show the audience in a theatre.   .

Therefore, while a play script should be mostly dialogue and little direction (in the majority of cases), a good screenplay is often the opposite. When you are writing a screenplay, the goal is to create a vivid visual experience for the reader. This is because you want a director or producer to read your screenplay and be able to imagine how the movie might look, which will make him or her excited about making your film.

Let's explore a brief sample from the screenplays of one of my favorite movies, *The Big Lebowski:*

```
BOWLING PINS

Scattered by a strike.

Music and head credits play over
various bowling shots—pins flying,
bowlers hoisting balls, balls gliding
down lanes, sliding feet, graceful
releases, ball return spinning up a
ball, fingers sliding into fingerholes,
etc.

The music turns into boomy source
music, coming from a distant jukebox,
as the credits end over a clattering
strike.

A lanky blonde man with stringy hair
tied back in a ponytail turns from the
strike to walk back to the bench.
```

```
                MAN
        Hot damn, I'm throwin' rocks
        tonight.

        Mark it, Dude.

We are tracking in on the circular
bench towards a big man nursing a large
plastic cup of Bud. He has dark worried
eyes and a goatee. Hairy legs emerge
from his khaki shorts. He also wears a
khaki army surplus shirt with the
sleeves cut off over an old bowling
shirt. This is Walter. He squints
through the smoke from his own
cigarette as he addresses the Dude at
the scoring table.
```

Do you see how the descriptions in between the dialogue are so descriptive and visual? This is an example of an excellent screenplay, written by acclaimed screenwriters and filmmakers, Joel and Ethan Coen.

Exercise

Write the screenplay for a short film or a scene within a longer film using minimal dialogue and focusing on making the descriptions as visual and filmic as possible.

Day Twenty-Six

Sound and Rhythm (Spoken Word)

"You can't really name a movement that didn't start with the spoken word."— Nancy Duarte

If you have ever been to a spoken word event, you understand how powerful it can be. Many people consider spoken word and poetry to be the same thing. This is certainly not the case. While poetry often works well when read aloud and spoken word often works well when read on the page, the art of writing a spoken word piece is different.

When crafting a spoken word piece, the way it looks on the page is a lot less important. You need to focus on the way that it sounds. It's important to pay attention to the rhythm of the words that you are using, your use of rhyme, and the vowel and consonant sounds that you use. Things like alliteration and consonance become important. When working on a spoken word piece, you must read it aloud.

Like plays, only half of the spoken word piece is the writing of it. The other half is performing it in front of an audience. When a great performer with commanding stage presence performs a spoken word piece, it can be captivating.

Exercise

Write a one to two minute spoken word piece. If possible, perform the piece live at an open mic night near you or record yourself performing the piece and upload it to YouTube.

Day Twenty-Seven

Follow Your Obsessions (Fan Fiction)

"Write the kind of story you would like to read.

People will give you all sorts of advice about writing,

but if you are not writing something you like, no one

else will like it either." — *Meg Cabot*

Fan fiction is very controversial. Many authors despise fan fiction and are adamantly against it. Others quite enjoy it. Whatever your thoughts on fan fiction, I'm asking you to suspend your personal beliefs and biases for one moment and just participate in this exercise with the idea that you are not going to publish this.

I'm definitely someone who gets obsessed with things. If you've ever sat through eight hours of *Dr. Who* episodes or stayed up all night reading *Harry*

Potter or you were depressed for two weeks after the Red Wedding episode of *Game of Thrones*, you know what I'm talking about.

There's a lot of talk about fan fiction and whether or not it has any validity. I think fan fiction is great because it gives people a chance to follow their obsessions. If you weren't happy with the werewolf imprinting on the baby vampire in *Breaking Dawn*, you can write a whole new version for yourself. If you're obsessed with Jack Skelington, you can write an epic story where he travels to New York City and gets stuck in Central Park. Often, fan fiction authors go on to write other original stories (*50 Shades of Grey* anyone? *The Mortal Instruments* series? Both of these came from fan fiction authors.)

In many cases, writers find their own voices by beginning with fan faction (as in *Fangirl* by Rainbow Rowell). Writing about something you are completely obsessed with may help you to find your own original characters and stories that will make you obsessed.

Exercise

Pick your absolute favorite book, movie, or TV show and write a short fan fiction story. The purpose of this exercise is to really dive into your obsessions so that you can get excited about storytelling and writing. Have fun with it and use your imagination!

Day Twenty-Eight

Imagination (Children's Books)

"There are some themes, some subjects, too large for adult fiction; they can only be dealt with adequately in a children's book." — *Philip Pullman*

Do you remember how vivid your imagination was when you were a kid? I remember playing all kinds of make-believe games with my friends when I was a child. I remember playing with dolls and stuffed animals and creating an entire world for each of my toys. I remember creating elaborate characters for them and writing stories all of the time. I remember when everything seemed magical, and the possibilities were endless.

Children's literature gives you a certain freedom that you don't have in adult books. This is not to say that you don't have to still follow the same rules of writing when creating children's books. You certainly do. However, you can be a lot more imaginative and create wonderful stories.

Think about your favorite children's books and movies and what makes them special. Is it the beautifully sad way that Peter Pan will never grow up? Is it the heartwarming family love expressed from Nemo's father? Is it the magical possibilities of Dr. Suess's *Oh, The Places You'll Go!?* For today's exercise, I'm asking you to re-connect with your inner child.

Exercise

Write a short story for children. Include illustrations if you are artistically inclined. Your story can be fantastical or realistic. It can be for children of any age up to 12. Go back to that time when everything was possible, and write a story you would

have loved as a child.

Day Twenty-Nine

World Building (Fantasy, Science Fiction, or Dystopian)

"Fantasy is hardly an escape from reality. It's a way of understanding it." — *Lloyd Alexander*

Today's exercise piggybacks on yesterday's exercise. When we write fantasy, science fiction, or dystopian, we are required to use that vivid imagination we had as children. You can do virtually anything in the fantasy, science fiction, and dystopian genres. These genres require you to build another world. This world can be similar to the world we currently live in or it can be entirely different.

Fantasy, science fiction, and dystopian literature are all excellent genres to use when you want to write in allegory or metaphor and say something about the society in which we live. In *1984,* George Orwell used a dystopian future to criticize communism and totalitarianism. Critics have drawn attention to Christian and Catholic themes in J.R.R. Tolkien's *The Lord of the Rings.* And who can forget that Douglas Adams gave us the answer to life, the universe, and everything in *The Hitchhiker's Guide to the Galaxy?*

Sometimes by stepping outside of our own world and creating a new world, we are able to write about a certain truth that we were unable to explore in the context of our own world. We can also do this while creating complex characters, interesting conflicts, and layers of fascinating literature as many dystopian, science fiction, and fantasy writers have done.

Exercise

Write a short story in either the dystopian, fantasy, or science fiction genre. Try to discuss something about our modern world that you believe in

119

strongly by creating a metaphor or allegory in one of these genres.

Day Thirty

Jump Off

"If there's a book that you want to read, but it hasn't been written yet, then you must write it." — *Toni Morrison*

Congratulations! You've made it to the last day of the 30-day writing challenge! Allow me to sum up all of the previous days in one sentence.

1. It doesn't matter what you write, just write.

2. Let go of the fear of writing something bad.

3. Write the story you want to write.

4. Use random prompts to get ideas when you get stuck.

5. Allow images to inspire you.

6. Allow great literature from other writers to inspire you.

7. Allow great music to inspire you.

8. Allow great visual art to inspire you and support other artists.

9. Go for a walk or look outside.

10. Change your writing location for a new experience.

11. Use outlines and organization to structure your plot.

12. Concentrate on vocabulary and word choice.

13. Get to know your characters inside and out.

14. Use varied sentence structures in your writing.

15. Focus on creating dialogue that is true to the way people speak.

16. Revise, revise, revise. Then revise some more.

17. Think about the point of view you are using to tell the story.

18. Give the readers clues and hints.

19. Do your research.

20. Complete the story. Make sure it has a beginning, middle, and end.

21. Be true to yourself and your story.

22. Use memorable images. Show the reader what you mean, don't just tell him.

23. Understand the unspoken subtext your characters are thinking.

24. Give your characters layers and complexity.

25. Visualize. See your stories happening.

26. Pay attention to rhythm, consonance, alliteration, and the way the words sound.

27. Follow your obsessions.

28. Connect with your inner child, your inner innocence.

29. Use your imagination.

These are all great rules to follow if you want to create compelling writing. But you don't need to follow all of these rules in everything you write. These are simply guidelines. It's wonderful to practice different aspects of writing and push yourself to grow as a writer, but at the end of the day, you can do whatever you want. You can write whatever you want, and I encourage you to do just that.

My hope is that these exercises have helped you to either start a new daily writing habit or strengthen the writing habit that you already have. My hope is that many of these exercises opened you up to a new way of writing and have inspired you to try something new. My hope is that you complete this challenge with a better understanding of why you love the books you love and an understanding that will help you to write books other people will love (or plays, screenplays, poems, stories, etc.).

Exercise

Today's exercise is to take any of the previous exercises and use it as a jumping off point to create a wonderful short story, novel, screenplay, play, collection of poems, non-fiction piece, spoken word piece, or any other form of writing. You should not try to complete this in one day, but rather continue to work on this piece over time until it is polished and you feel great about it. At that point, I encourage you (very much!) to submit your piece for publication or production. Get it out there. Share it with others. Do not keep your stories inside of you. You have a unique voice and a unique story to tell in a way that no one else can. So go out there and tell it in the best way you can.

Acknowledgements

Special thanks to Shaunnon Drake, Arlen Crawford, and Melanie Stephens for the editing, feedback, and advice.

Thank you to all of the writing professors, teachers, and mentors who have taught me everything I know about creative writing and art, Billie Shook, Steven Jones, Gavin Karstensen, Dr. David King, Dr. Keith Botelho, Dr. Craig Watson, Addae Moon, James Winter, Henry Griffin, and Bill Lavender, to name a few.

Thank you to Mom and Dad for always giving me the opportunities to pursue my writing and supporting me.

Join the Find Creative Expression community!

Sign up for the weekly mailing list, listen to the podcast, and join the Facebook group at

findcreativeexpression.com

Thank you so much for supporting indie authors! If you have enjoyed this book, please take a moment to leave a review on your favorite book retailer. And please join my mailing list at **saracrawford.net!**

Sara Crawford Official Website
saracrawford.net

Find Creative Expression Blog and Podcast
findcreativeexpression.com

Instagram
instagram.com/saraecrawford

Twitter
twitter.com/sara_crawford

Facebook
facebook.com/saracrawfordmusic

YouTube
youtube.com/saracrawford

About the Author

Sara Crawford is an author, playwright, and musician from Marietta, Georgia. She has an MFA in Playwriting from the University of New Orleans and a BA in English from Kennesaw State University. She is also the host of the Find Creative Expression podcast (findcreativeexpression.com – also available on Spotify, Apple, Google Podcasts, etc.), conversations about art and creativity. She lives with her cat, Julian. For more information, visit https://saracrawford.net.

Other Books by Sara Crawford
Saracrawford.net/books

The Muse Chronicles Trilogy

The Shadow Vampires Trilogy

Time After Time

Poetry Collections

13480050R00080